Keep your hopes
and dreams alive
Jack Marschall

Love is The Bond

HappyJack
Publishing™

HappyJack Publishing
P.O. Box 30363 • Middleburg Heights, Ohio 44130

Marschall, Jack P.

Circle of Life:
A book of rhymes on the funny, serious and
even sad realities of life. It's a glimpse in the mirror at
living, laughing and loving. / Jack P. Marschall.

ISBN 0-9729672-1-4

Printed in the United States by Cleveland Business Forms
Layout and Design by Digital Impressions, Inc.

For more information: HappyJackPubs.com

DEDICATION

This book is dedicated to those who helped me
realize my dreams with constructive criticism,
support, inspiration and the magic of love.
Thanks for believing in me.

To my loving wife Sharon,
my children Eric, Sarah, Adam,
Lauren, my family and friends.

To my best friend, teacher
and father, Peter A. Marschall.

It's Me

One thing in this world
I honestly hate
Are people who think
They're awesome and great

The brag about this
They talk about that
It's all about ME
And I and MY crap

They're bloated with ego
It could burst at the seam
Because all their life
They had but one dream

To let everyone know
How important they are
The absolute truth?
They never went far

Real power to me
Is so quiet and tame
To care about others
Attracts real fame

It draws no attention
You're never too loud
You seldom get noticed
Or stand out in a crowd

There's no need to brag
Cause whatever you do
If it's really good stuff
They'll find out that it's you

The folks who carry on
About things they have done
Are those you walk far from
And in some cases run

Measure the greatness
When people go by
They care about others
Never brag about "I"

TRASH TV

Did you ever look
At daytime TV?
Wow, I'm in shock
What my baby eyes see

They still have soap operas
More risqué than before
Old boring game shows
Win a car, maybe more

But I nearly dropped
One talk show to the next
The bleepin' and fightin'
Left me quite perplexed

This one is married
To that sister's boy
But she's still in love
With her brother, Roy

They take off their clothes
Like it's something brand new
And I guess that's the case
Cause it's quarter past two

People are screamin'
The guests punch and swear
I might like what's said
If they had more to wear

This circus is crazy
To those with a brain
When did shows like this start?
Who's at fault, who's to blame?

Then I had a great thought
The power is mine
I pushed on the clicker
Now I'm feeling fine

The lesson is simple
You may even know
If you hate that TV
Find a much better show

But don't sit and complain
About all the buffoons
As for me, I'm switching
To my favorite cartoons

Heaven's Sake

I wonder where is heaven?
Why is it we don't know?
If we're good when we die
Then where is it that we go?

So what does it look like?
Where is it we would stay?
Is it just around the corner?
Or way up there, far away?

I hope to see my mother
When it comes my time to leave
I'm not assuming anything
It takes much more than PLEASE!

I have a very strong feeling
That heaven is right here
The place where we're now living
Minus hate and wars and fear

What I say you've heard before
Live each day as your last
Be nice to others and to you
Don't dwell much on the past

The golden rule is on the mark
Treat all as they should treat you
And if you stay on this course
The world to come will be new

It may not be up in the clouds
With angels flying on high
Life after death is here on earth
Graduation, the day you die

Look around, here you'll stay
Heaven is not up above
The way it was meant to be
A world with eternal love

Timeless Love

The joys of my life
In one word or two
Are things that brought me
Much closer to you

Miracle or destiny
Luck or even fate
They're reasons for living
Our union, so great

How did it happen?
A gift such as you
No, never any choosing
I never thought about "who"

We were kids at the start
Young, filled with fright
Partners for a moment
Partners for life

Riches then followed
Kids of our own
Miracles to witness
More love in our home

Always you'd give
Showed me the way
In our times of sorrow
We'd pray every day

Our bond is not perfect
It's one normal life
The difference is having
You as my wife

GOING HOME

There's a man on the street
That all my buddies like
Kinda dirty, kind of strange
Never causes any fights

Wears clothes like a soldier
Says, "Hey, they're all mine."
He tells those who'll listen
"I make rhymes for a dime."

I said hi, "My name is Jack,
Tell a tale about me."
He said, "Jack, you're a gift
Seeing good in those you see.

You're nice, true and honest
You're caring, you behave
Your parents must be proud
You've always been so brave."

The man laughed and clapped
My buddies said, "pay up!"
So I dropped a new dime
In his rusty old cup

My friends did not know
This guy was a fighter
He was once young like us
So many pounds lighter

He told stories of war
A place called Vietnam
Sounds quiet and peaceful
So foreign, yet so calm

He talked of seeing death
Many parts he can't tell
Said it was so scary
Looked, smelled just like hell

The sadness and the pain
See it on his face
He spent almost two years
In that faraway place

Many friends never went
Some had school, others ran
He said men made choices
Condemned no one's life plan

This bright, aging man
Fought for who knows why
Came home with no glory
Came back a different guy

He struggles just to live
To look like any man
From one street to the next
With that old rusty can

I could have given-up
Gone to school, no goodbye
But he was part of me
We needed so to cry

I walked right up the street
With my prayers, not a dime
Told him that I loved him
I didn't want a rhyme

"It's time to come home, dad.
I know the pain's still there.
Please give it one more chance.
We'll help you clear the air.

"Mom cries as much as you
She's coping every day
Her pain I've tried to help
Love never went away."

Tears fell from his face
His cup dropped to the ground
"I've wondered who I am.
Today, I think I'm found."

I grabbed his hand and face
To try and keep him strong
"Dad, it's time to come back.
You've done nothing wrong.

"You kept us safe before.
We missed you all the time.
Breaks our hearts to see you.
Making rhymes for a dime.

"We'll try to pay you back
With love, more than you know."
He said, there is one truth,
"Your love, your care has shown."

We hugged and walked away
To our house near the mall
A laugh, a cry, a bear hug
Like when I was so small

I loved dad as a kid
Love him more as a man
Lost in war with demons
Now has his life-long plan

Today he looks real good
I call, we talk by phone
Mom calls it a miracle
Dad needed to come home

MELINDA MAE GLASS

This lady I know
Melinda Mae Glass
Had a terrible smell
My mom said is gas

When she came by
You could hear putt-putt
Directly from, well
I think you know what

Miss Glass was so happy
She'd laugh when she smelled
She thought it was funny
Said "I'm ringin' the bells."

I never could face it
Her odor or sounds
I prayed and made sure
I was never around

But one day I slept
On the couch when she came
The bells they were banging
The smell like a flame!

It's Melinda Mae Glass
Making music that rings
Thank goodness for us
She never learned how to sing

Father's Day

I'm the only son
He's the only dad
He'd always be there
On days I was bad

Working countless jobs
Seldom seen or heard
Still, always present
Reassuring words

I never got the plan
I never sat and talked
We never had the time
I'd be myself and walk

And all through the years
So deep was his faith
It was unspoken love
Shared by holy grace

Fleeting time for me
My kids fully grown
No time to sit and talk
They're now on their own

I always wanted more
Not money or fame
Just some peace of mind
In life's hectic game

I gave them advice
Wrapped tightly with love
Just like my dad
The faith from above

The plan was right there
I thought it to be bad
A reality check
I've become my dad

Something I would dread
Now a source of pride
My father's legacy
A loving, peaceful tide

CLOCK TALK

Tick and tock
Goes the clock
The hands fly 'round like a fan

And we always say
I'll do it my way
Today or whenever I can

We often assume
Tomorrow will bloom
Others we'll look for and find

We never expect
To one day regret
We didn't do more with our time

Seconds fill up
Like sand in a cup
Gushing into years and a day

It's so crystal clear
See truthfulness near
To hear it as well as to say

The words we could speak
So soothing, so meek
I'm sad for the hurt that you feel

To hear the same thing
Like the magic it brings
Works wonders to make our wounds heal

It's easy to do
I've no time for you
Just wait 'till I'm ready, not now

You know that's not truth
Like tales from our youth
Be the one to show others how

Be wise with your time
It's neither yours nor mine
It arrives and then flies away

Make peace as your grow
Forgive and let go
Feel the love at the end of the day

Circle of Life

Little boys
Little girls
Little clothes
Little curls

Bubble baths
Dirty jeans
Broken bats
Jelly beans

Feeding ducks
Washing hands
Rocking babies
Castles of sand

Wishing wells
School bus rides
T-ball games
Run and hide

Doctor visits
Sleepless nights
Fevers high
Sibling fights

Confirmation
Graduations
Temper tantrums
Destinations

Babies grown
Leaving home
Changing lives
All alone

Getting older
Wedding days
Babies born
Grandkids raised

Little boys
Little girls
Little clothes
Little curls

Generations
Husband and wife
Beautiful sunsets
Circle of life

FAT CAT

I knew this old bag
She was fat like a cat
Shook the ground walking
Left marks where she sat

Paws, claws and whiskers
She hissed when she fell.
And when she got hungry
She'd howl, scream and yell

This lady was so hairy
So scary and so wide
The neighbors would run
And find places to hide

But that's not the worst
About this wild crazy cat
She had a skinny old husband
Who looked just like a rat

He too had big whiskers
Long teeth and a snout
Now there's no doubting
What this tale's all about

The fat lady's the boss
Her husband's a louse
He would squeak, bite and jump
Acting more like a mouse

Why they were married
No one knows or cares
They're gone from our street
And their stories we share

Our guess is they screamed
And they kicked and they spat
And we bet that fat lady
Gobbled-up that skinny rat

MOMMA'S BOY

I'm as tough
As tough can be
All my friends
Are afraid of me

I yell and kick
I scream and punch
I beat-up sissies
Just for lunch

I'm mean and green
I always win
The kids all say
Stay far from him

I howl and laugh
When people run
I love to see me
Spoil their fun

I can't believe
The things I do
I scare myself
I'd scare you, too

I'm big and tough
As tough can be
But gotta run –
Momma's calling me!

HAPPY SOCKS

There's a place in a drawer
In a spot where it's dark
Where I live by myself
I'm one very ugly sock

My friends are all pairs
Folded nice and neat
I'm just a lonely sock
No one else to meet

I sit there by myself
Hope my twin will come
That was weeks ago
I'm still me – just one

It might be in the hall
In the top of a box
Maybe gone forever
The land of mismatched socks

I hear someone coming
With an armful of clothes
Putting some above me
Does anybody know?

Shoved aside every time
Wrinkled, squished away
I can't believe, what's this
She came for me that day!

From the top of the socks
From the top of the clothes
She pulls out my lost mate
Wraps him tight 'round my toes

Boy, it's good to see you
You're out of that big box
We're now back together
No longer separate socks!

NEW DIRECTIONS

So many hopes
So many schemes
So many choices
So many dreams

So many wishes
So many wonders
So many victories
So man blunders

So many plans
So many years
So many joys
So many tears

So many hurts
So many loves
So many vultures
So many doves

So many chances
So many ways
So many questions
So many days

So many people
So many lives
So many feelings
So many tides

So many answers
So many whys
So many truths
So many lies

So many needs
So many fires
So many maybes
So many desires

So many heavens
So many hearts
So many pieces
So many parts

So many watching
So many wait
So many praying
So many late

So many come
So many go
So many high
So many low

So many give
So many take
So many love
So many hate

So many travel
So many roam
So many together
So many alone

So many see
So many call
So many lead
So many fall

So many ifs
So many flows
So many yeses
So many no's

So many miles
So many reasons
So many smiles
So many seasons

So many hopes
So many schemes
So many choices
So many dreams

BABE ESCAPE

I got so mad
I ran away
I told them both
Don't talk that way

I may be small
I'm not that tall
But you forgot
I'm good to crawl

I looked around
And jumped right down
I turned my legs
And went to town

My hands and feet
Moved fast, how sweet
And look-eee here
I've got them beat

With all my might
I'm outta sight
They won't find me
Till late tonight

I'll never show
Which way I'll go
But this strange room
I do not know

It's big and dark
Is that a bark?
Let's just forget
Their last remark

They're still so young
Their baby son
They just forgot
That I can run

Now what was that
Our hungry cat?
And look at me
So big and fat!

My legs are froze
My fingers, toes
Can't budge an inch
My nightmare grows!

I'm sick with fear
I'm way down here
That's a monster
Inside the mirror!

Look, it's creepy
Big and sleepy
Oh my gosh
I'm going pee-pee!

It's mom and dad
Am I so glad
I thought they left
Weren't they mad

But they're just fine
No worry, no whine
Smiling, laughing
Like all the time

I'm off the ground
I've now been found
We kiss and hug
No scary sounds

I'm in my chair
With food and Bear
I wonder why
I left their care

No more to say
A big, fun day
Just think before
You crawl away

PET PUZZLE

We have a cat
We have a dog
We have a bird
We have a frog

That may sound fine
To you and me
But something's strange
You're bound to see

Or should I say
You'll hear what's wrong
Millie the bird
Can't sing a song

What does she do?
She BARKS like Fred
I'm so ashamed
I hide my head

That's one pet down
And three to go
Freddie my dog
MEOWS real low!

I'm shocked and sad
You'll never know
That's two pets down
And two to go

My cat is Kate
And it's no joke
To talk real loud
She starts to CROAK!

I can't believe
This freaky show
That's three pets down
And one to go

Now this could be
The worst of all
My frog Miguel
CHIRPS when I call!

My pets all look
So strange, this thing
Miguel looks like
A frog with wings

Poor Fred is cute
Happy and fat
His face and paws
Look like a cat

Millie can't fly
Sits like a log
Watch closely now
She looks a dog

I can't complain
My pets are nice
But if you want
Take my advice

My pets are fun
To have around
Only wish they made
The proper sounds!

Being You

If you ever fix a stare
At someone in the face
Be careful not to wish
You'd love to take their place

They may look real happy
Super healthy, extra fine
Your life may be driving you
Completely out of your mind

There's something very holy
Very sacred and it's true
As bad as things may get
There is only one of you

That man there lost his wife
Died of cancer, loss of love
That girl there lost her mom
In a plane that flew above

That baby lost her daddy
In a fight inside a bar
That lady lost her grandkids
In the crash of their new car

The nice man just stopped crying
An hour or two ago
After drugs gave his boy
Only one bad way to go

That couple with the kids
Not a care upon their face
They'd do anything at all
If YOU would take their place

They look happy and care-free
About the best that you can
After losing one great father
One amazingly good man

So try to be as pleased
With your life, luck and home
As tough as things may get
You are never all alone

Life is one big miracle
One to truly behold
It's there to keep and cherish
Like a piece of priceless gold

The faith, strength and hope
Will get you through the dark
Getting past the painful times
Leaves us stronger, leaves our mark

Others also struggle
They have pain, sad but true
But stay strong to be yourself
Cause there's only one of you

MESSY MARTHA

When I was small
And bored and blue
I'd tell my mom
There's nothing to do

Nowhere to go
No one to see
I'd whine and cry
"I want to be free."

"You're free as a bird,"
Mom said with a glare
"Go see that girl
With all the hair.

"She's nice and pretty
She's good and smart
You might learn something
If you don't watch out."

So then I gave in
What to do or say
Went to Mary Martha
For more than one day

I did not like her
She looked like a mess
"I'm called Messy Martha,"
She quickly confessed

Her hair was snarly
Her figure was fat
She seemed so friendly
And always, always sat

The girl was simple
Plain and very smart
Said nice things to me
Happy from the start

Mary was so kind
So nice, not scared
She too had a mom
Who was nice, who cared

"I do it all myself
I do it all the time
Dress and brush my hair
To be proud and feel fine."

Then I looked at Mary
Like never before
She was so very different
So brave and not a bore

She said I was lucky
Fun to have around
A mom to keep me safe
My feet on the ground

But then Mary Martha
Had words in her eyes
Said she too was lucky
Happy and so wise

She talked and talked
Brushed her hair again
Her face then lit up
Spoke of life without end

The more we talked
The more I could see
Martha wasn't messy
Her dream was to be free

She was proud and brave
Not lost for a smile
We became best friends
For quite a long while

We both grew up quickly
Traveled over time
Mary would still be there
Very easy to find

She died before college
It made us very sad
The only thing that Mary
Ever had that was bad

Such a good teacher
About love and life
She sat and talked
Shared worldly advice

Mary was my sister
I miss her and I cry
Years before I cared
Time that flew right by

She was my best friend
Gave me love, wit and truth
Now I know just why
She laughed at our youth

Known as Messy Martha
Lived without our help
Touched all who met her
Just by being herself

A sister that I loved
One for whom I cared
She made herself pretty
Tiny brush, messy hair

Snow Ride

It was one of those days
I should have stayed home
The snow was piling high
And I was all alone

I had the bright idea
To leave and buy some bread
Maybe milk and cookies
Cheese and a dozen eggs

So why go out right now
With a blinding storm of white?
"It'll be fine," I said bravely
Though I knew it wasn't right

I confess I had the urge
Kinda felt like one big dare
I never scare that easy
So I don't really care

I got right in my car
Like a soldier at war
Slid sideways out the drive
I was laughing for more

But only minutes away
From my toasty warm home
My choices seemed so dumb
Yea, it was stupid to roam

I arrived at the store
As I screamed like a girl
Slipping sideways and back
And swirling in those curls

I bought what I needed
Started back once again
Saw cars parked, abandoned
I think I saw my friend

I know this was crazy
I continued to drive
"I have food – I have God,
I know that I'll survive!"

I let out one loud shrill
A whimper and a sigh
The car was doing things
That made this grown man cry

Control left my body
My car, it slid some more
This time rocking, socking
My poor head hit the floor

I was stopped in the middle
Of a dark and scary street
Still alone and now so cold
Others home with all their heat

I came to my senses
I decided to walk
Made it home half frozen
Looked like human chalk

I warmed-up my fingers
And fired-up the grill
I thought my poor, cold body
Would never lose the chill

The drama and the fright
I survived, started shakin'
I whispered this to God
"We forgot to buy the bacon!"

SNORE WARS

I love my wife dearly
She's pretty and smart
We laugh each day of the week

There's nothing I'd change
Not one blessed thing
Never would dare even tweak

She loves me so dearly
And I love her right back
Seems we will always be one

But now that you ask
I'd have to admit
One thing is not lots of fun

My queen of a wife
Has only one fault
Not bad and who's keeping score?

When she closes her eyes
In our quiet bedroom
She lets out a big ol' SNORE

It's tiny at first
She falls fast asleep
Has no clue where she's at

But in no time at all
The volume goes up
I put on my anti-snore hat

It's red, white and blue
With flaps on the side
To cushion my ears and my head

In one, two and three
The snoring gets LOUD
It's now even moving our bed

I have no complaints
'Bout this tiny one fault
My wife doesn't even know why

I push and I shove
Her side and her arms
Till she jumps and opens her eyes

"Why's the bed here?
A hat on your head?
Are you drunk or just being cute?"

She closes her eyes
I grab the remote
And keep on hitting the MUTE

Night Flight

The pain you've had so long
Is something we all feel
You can see it on your face
It's crude and God, so real

Where does it come from?
There's no way you can hide
It doesn't really matter
We're with you for the ride

We were there last night
The mood, sick and mean
You, the kids and babies
The yelling turned to screams

Countless times to run away
For you, those in your care
Leave behind the threats and hate
Escape is no longer a dare

Survival is the goal of life
Respect and love the key
Don't stay and see your life destroyed
Grab the babies, don't wait, just flee

We're holding your hands
We're out in the car
Come with us quickly
You need to go far

The horror is so real
It's sad and deadly, too
We're there in your escape
We care what happens to you

FuZZy WuZZy

I once had hair
On top of my head
Now it's just fuzz
It almost looks dead

I comb it over here
Toss it over there
But when I'm all done
It doesn't look like hair

I count all my strands
There's one, two, three, four
I used to have five
Oh, but not anymore

I'd shave my head clean
But it looks so darn square
Without patchy fuzz
It would cause a big scare

I could wear a wig
Pretend that it's mine
But I'd look like a girl
Just to cover the shine

A toupee would look good
But then people would stare
Saying, look at that rug
That's not his real hair

I once had a thought
To put paint on my head
But that would be sloppy
When I'd go off to bed

I try not to figure
What I don't have and why
I just cover my head
And let out one big sigh

I've got a nice smile
Personality's great
I'm just about perfect
Except for one small trait

The locks I once had
Decided now to leave
I'm stuck with my looks
And what people perceive

I don't feel that bad
It can always be worse
I could wear a helmet
Or hide behind a purse

I could have a nose
That was big, round and fat
Or a couple of ears
That were made for a rat

I could have big teeth
In the back of my neck
Bony fingers like claws
And eyes like, what the heck

All that I'm missing
Is hair for my top
It's not that big a deal
My complaining, I'll stop

Still, I sometimes wonder
When I glance in the mirrors
What would I look like
With long hair past my ears?

Those days are long gone
Still, I'm not feeling bad
Just wondering "hey, what if"
I still had what I once had

BONUS Baby

Tears in my eyes
Hope in my heart
News of a baby
Shock from the start

Our baby's the mom
So young and alive
So worried we are
How can she survive?

Anger and sadness
Emotions overflow
Questions, no answers
Where will she go?

Then it begins
It falls into place
Love that we share
With beauty and grace

Far from within
The truth shines through
Sharing big hugs
It's all about you

One day at a time
Is the best advice
Giving all we have
Never thinking twice

It's more than a test
Defines who we are
It's our way of life
A burning night star

It won't be easy
Dreams put on hold
What God created
Will live in the fold

Faith is the answer
Strength from above
Given as we said
Unconditional love

FREEDOM FIGHTER

You can own a house
You can own a boat
You can own the water
Buy a ship and float

You can own a car
You can own a suit
You can own a store
Buy a farm with fruit

Possessions are so great
Making us feel strong
But owning someone's life?
Impossible and wrong!

Surviving is tough
Working for the boss
No rewards or smiles
Only fear, hate and loss

Live the golden rule
Always give respect
Do it now and always
Live life without regret

Freedom we all own
It's given during birth
It's for the rich and poor
For all of us on earth

You can't own a person
We're not puppets, we're free
Pass around some dignity
You certainly don't own me

SCREAM TEAM

I asked my daddy
If he would scream
It sounded just like
A washin' machine

I asked my mommy
If she would yell
It sounded just like
A deep hollow well

I asked my sister
If she would squeal
It sounded just like
A rusty old wheel

I asked my brother
If he would growl
It sounded just like
A sick friendly owl

I asked my grandma
If she would roar
And oh my goodness
She fell on the floor

I asked my grandpa
If he would snarl
He tried and he laughed
Popped his teeth in a towel

I ask all these folks
To make funny sounds
I like when they laugh
When no one's around

They laugh more than me
It's a game for them, too
The noises they make
You can hear at the zoo

But THIS game is easy
You stay right at home
It can even be great
If you play it alone

Squeal, snort and scream
I do them quite well
I practice a lot
Make sure you don't tell

If they all find out
I'm better than them
They'd get real quiet
The game would soon end

They just couldn't take it
Not a yell, growl or roar
So I think just for them
I'll keep playing some more

SICK SALLY

Small Sally is sick
She hurts and she aches
The pain, it gets her down

So she slept on the couch
Gave her body a rest
Then fell hard to the ground

She rolled like a ball
Till the dog helped her up
She thought her feet were OK

Two cats who were near
Caused Sally great fear
So she rolled the other darn way

The bird in the cage
Screamed and he yelled
"Get up and do this yourself."

So small Sally grabbed
For the arm of the chair
Standing like some drunken elf

She took one step then two
Looked down at her foot
Caught on her little pet snake

She slipped and she flew
Like the bird in the cage
And landed on top of a cake

Wide Sally was sticky
And gooey and sweet
Looked like a birthday bad wish

If only she had
A neat helping hand
She looked at her tiny pet fish

Their eyes grew with grief
But Sally knew best
The bowl was for balance and poise

"Not a good idea,"
Said the fish with a swish
Sally crashed, making more noise

She finally woke up
It was all just a dream
She yawned and looked on the floor

What she couldn't explain
Was the mess in the room
Her crazy pets begging for more!

On that very day
Sally learned to be smart
Careful, don't bruise your big head

So now when she's sick
The pets stay away
Sally stays tucked in her bed

Fun Run

Remember when running
Was done just for fun?
I'd run through the house
Or out in the sun

I'd run to the store
For my mom or my dad
My sisters would run
To punch me, they were bad

Running was always
A big part of life
Until I got older
And ran after my wife

The kids bloomed like flowers
One, two, three then four.
I'd always be working
Running out the door

The kids grew-up quickly
Before my own eyes
And so did my belly
My behind and my thighs

So then it was time
To look back in the mirror
What I saw made me scream
And caused me great fear

I yelled and I stomped
And I finally cried
"I look like a blimp,
I'm as big as the sky!"

I saw this nice man
With no hair on his head
Big belly, big butt
I was more than well-fed

Who IS this wide man?
Gosh, he looks oh so fat
"Get out of my house
And don't ever come back."

He just looked in my eyes
Cracked a smile and a frown
It was me who had grown
To the size of our town

So what in the world
Can you do to lose weight?
Well, jumping and biking
I could learn how to skate

Where this is going?
You've got to go run
But as you get old
There's sweat, cramps and fun???

A treadmill I run on
As I stare in the mirror
And as I get older
One thing I hold dear

That the fat, aging man
Who sweats when he runs
Will forget the sore aches
And remember the fun

Laughing Medicine

Bill's in the hospital
He's been pretty sick
The doctors are helping
But nothing does the trick

They're so gloomy and dark
So depressing and sad
They do more harm than good
I'd say they're even bad

And then I showed-up
And shoved everyone out
To make my friend smile
To laugh and even shout

I told Bill some jokes
That got such a rise
He sat up and howled
Like he'd won some great prize

He talked as he laughed
He shook his big head
And laughed even louder
After wetting the bed

I'd try my own magic
The whole time I'm there
In a couple more weeks
He was out of their hair

The doctors have names
For what Bill had and why
Names for the medicine
The cost was so high

I know that my magic
Was better than the staff's
All I did was show love
Some smiles and some laughs

SMOKE SCREEN

There is something so sad
About smoking cigarettes
Cancer and the coughing
Emphysema, the sweats

So many huff 'n puffers
They'd do anything to quit
But the people who make 'em
Know that causes smokers fits

I thought that addiction
Was just in your mind
Those who couldn't quit
Were just weak all the time

Then my kids and my friends
Got hooked on that smoke
And it didn't take long
Before they'd cough and choke

It made me try and help
But nothing I could say
Would make 'em stop puffin'
Make their coughs go away

Now I pray that one day
They'll find strength to quit
And live a healthier life
Not squirming in a fit

I pray for those smart folks
Making cancer sticks look cool
They make tons of money
Making all of us the fool

If there's justice after life
And they meet ol' St. Peter
He'll blow smoke in their face
Push them down in the HEATER

Their suffering's not bad
More like one bitter pill
For all the people they duped
The ones they sickened and killed

MASTER PLAN

I often wonder what I'll do
When I go from a kid to a man
Maybe something really cool
There's more that I can't than I can

I never learned to fix those things
I'm better at tearing apart
I could paint it nice and new
But who would buy my art?

My job will make bad things better
In a world where help seems to fade
I would try to give the have-nots
And their kids great things I made

There's one thing I've discovered
What I'd do won't make me a star
The art in life is giving yourself
A plan that takes everyone far

Money is king, legacy green
We can't see the future in time
So change someone else's life
It makes sense to give them our time

GARBAGE GHOSTS

Why does my garbage stink
I wonder why it smells
I ask the guys who pick it up
But they say they'll never tell

The truck rolls down the street
The garbage tossed in the back
Why do they touch it, yuck?
Stinky bugs it doesn't lack

See the critters out at night
They tear our garbage to shreds
What could be in big black bags
It smells like something dead

Garbage scares me every time
It catches me off guard
Out my window late at night
I see garbage ghosts in my yard

They pick, smell, take what they want
They're loud and always so slow
This or that they'll stick in their sack
And then after hours they'll go

These pickers are smart, very neat
They know what they need and why
And if it doesn't stink enough
The garbage ghosts begin to cry

Make sure you wrap your garbage up
Keep it locked and bundled tight
You don't want those garbage ghosts
Having a smelly party at night

PLAY BALL!

Baseball should be played
When it's cozy and warm
Not when it's cold
And not in a storm

My ears are fallin' off
My frosty face is froze
Oh, take a look right now
I just broke my icy nose

I cannot see a thing
My big umbrella broke
Baseball in the rain
Is not a funny joke

I can't move my fingers
I can hardly move my feet
I'd pay a million bucks
For a nice blast of heat

My leg is numb and wet
Don't want to tell you why
The reason is, I fear
Would make a grown man cry

Everyone keeps playing
And that's a silly shame
Why don't the guys in blue
Quickly call this frozen game?

My kid is up at bat
And look, she got a hit
She's hugging both her hands
The pain is causing fits

The score is not too close
We're winning by a bunch
I don't really give a hoot
Cause I just lost my lunch!

Finally back inside my car
There's just one inning more
Now the feeling's coming back
I think I'll run to the store

Have to buy new ears and nose
I need some pills for pain
I'll never watch a game again
In the cold and freezing rain

By the way, my kid's team won
They told me on the phone
I'm meeting them to celebrate
They're buying ice cream cones!

DOWN UNDER

Graveside markers
Across the lot
Folks underneath
Still say a lot

Knitting in the winter
Reading books in June
Living inside a box
Under a shiny moon

Sounds kinda spooky
Sounds kinda weird
They're very friendly people
Who take away the fear

Good Sean Morganson
The loudest and so tall
Telling jokes of Ireland
Sharing pints with one and all

Harry and Larry Tucker
The brothers who fought crime
Gunned-down in Chicago
Now they're only killing time

There's Tom and Mrs. Green
Came here after a fight
Now they joke about life
Stay up 'till the morning light

It's not exactly heaven
Not bad enough for hell
Kinda like a weigh station
With friends, family and smells

One day soon the call will come
To tell where each will go
Till then pass the pints and cards
Let's guess who's next to show

PIZZA PARTY

Upon leaving this place
On the day that I die
I have one final wish
To eat hot pizza pie

Oh sure, I will cry
Prepare if I can
Thinking and hoping
For one deep dish pan

Ate pizza all my life
Made by my late friend Tom
On my last day with you
I'll have cheese sticks around

Extra sauce would be nice
Cheese bread if there's time
It's so very special
Could I please have some wine?

There's much more to life
Than dough, cheese and sauce
But this stuff is so good
In heaven, Tom's the boss!

BEE BUDDY

Did you ever see
How fast I run?
I'm like a bullet
Shot from a gun

I take a hike
The speed of sound
I do all this
When no one's around

I scare some folks
All half to death
They try but fail
To catch their breath

I think it's good
That they not see
Why I'm so fast
Yep, I'm a bee!

I buzz around
I fly and dive
I'm off again
To my surprise

Can't stand the thought
To hurt or sting
I like to fly
That's my best thing

People and pets
All run away
Whenever I swoop
Too close, they say

"Look out, a bee
He'll bite and sting
Go get that can
The bee spray thing."

They're not that mean
They're scared of buzzzz
They jump and squirm
And just because

My buzzing friends
Enjoy the bite
They aim and fire
With stinging delight

I try and warn
The folks I like
And my alarm
Is buzzzzz, no bite

But by the time
They hear my call
They jump and run
They sometimes fall

Now I can't speak
For every bee
But look real close
You'll recognize me

I'm the only one
Who smiles and flies
And now hear this
You'll be surprised

There's nothing to do
When I buzz on by
Just give me that cool
Buzzin' bee high five!

You won't regret
The nice hello
I'm not concerned
With who's below

Let me fly
Around all day
And keep away
That nasty spray

We may be friends
Best friends, real quick
No need to worry
My stinger's been fixed

Coaster Kid

The most fun I ever had
Was riding rides at the park
When I was so young and alive

My favorite was riding
That roller coaster thing
On that I could barely survive

This one was so rough
It would throw me around
Like a bug in a zapping machine

But I really didn't care
I was young and not scared
Even though it was fast, loud and mean

I think that the coaster
Was trying to prove
It was stronger and tougher than me

So I kept on riding
Hanging on for dear life
To prove nothing could zap my strength free

The last ride of the night
My stomach, it hurt
And began to spin round and round

And as hard as I tried
I couldn't take this dumb ride
I got off and fell to the ground

No, I didn't throw-up
And I didn't back down
I just walked away one, two three

And now that I'm older
I like WATCHING the rides
Being dizzy and sick's not for me

VAN MAN

We always had a big ol' car
With ten kids it was awfully tight
But dad would always tell us
"For today, right now, it's alright."

We all grew-up and got bigger
The big car got real, real small
And pretty soon all of us kids
Were looking and feeling too tall

We'd all get in and ride to school
Sitting on seats and the floor
And we'd all hang on for dear life
So we wouldn't fly out of the door

One day a big surprise and dream
Dad came home with a huge blue can
The cash he had saved forever
To buy us a neat, bright new van!

The color we picked was red
The thing was as wide as our home
It gave us room to stretch our legs
It had TV and a phone

We drove it around forever
With dad right behind the wheel
He looked so smart, so strong and tall
OUR turn was not in the deal

Dad always said he'd show us how
He said it was easy and sleek
When we'd ask for van keys and money
He said not now, but maybe next week

The weeks and months went by so fast
We grumbled and said it's unfair
By the time we'd get the keys to drive
We wouldn't want to go anywhere

One day I know our dad won't fight
We'll take the big van in the drive
But I'll be ninety-four by then
My girlfriend will be ninety-five!

Wedding Day

I'm nervous and tired
I'm sleepy and wired
My kid gets married in the morning

I've taught him so well
As best I can tell
Doesn't need any kind of warning

He's smart and he's neat
He's quick on his feet
And tomorrow he'll say yes, I do

It's time to let go
Let him have his own show
I've told him it's now up to you

The father of the groom
Is like the bristles on a broom
Just hangin' in case someone calls

So I'll be nice and polite
Try to break-up any fights
Hope my dancing won't cause any falls

A big day for my boy
Filled with tears and much joy
Another hour has passed right by

My only hope is to sleep
And to dream of his leap
The groom's dad is going to cry

UNLUCKY ME

I've had a bad year
So please go away
There's nothing to see
And nothing to say

I'm bitter and grumpy
And I think you'd be, too
If all that happened
Was happening to you

I bought a new car
That died in a week
Worse than a lemon
The fluids would leak

I bought a new home
That looked like a charm
But after the fire
It looks more like a barn

I got a new job
It paid lots of cash
The stocks, making millions
Till the market went CRASH!

I met a nice lady
She called me her honey
Loved each other dearly
She left with my money

I'm back to just me
And it's me all alone
There's not too much left
They just took out my phone

I think if there's hope
It's doing all you can
To make sense of the mess
Be strong and be a man!

The only thing to do
Is keep your fingers crossed
Head in the same direction
As for me, I'm a little lost

So Tired

Another yawn
Another day
Feel so tired
I'll sleep till May

My eyes are closed
My feet, they move
I'm walking now
A Frankenstein snooze

Folks all scream
When I come near
Now they're running
What do they fear?

I tell them stop
I will not bite
I like my walks
During the night

I'm on the street
The bats fly by
They too will scream
I don't know why

Cats and dogs
And skunks and flies
Make funny sounds
To open my eyes

I stretch and tug
My eyes stay shut
It looks like I'm stuck
A sleepwalking rut

Now wait a sec
Here's what I'll do
I'll count to three
And feel like new

First, on one
The nasty skunk
Let's one loose
Boy, am I'm sunk

How about two?
The big old dog
Growls, bites down
In a smoky fog

How about three?
The scary cat
Claws so nasty
I just lay flat

Now back in bed
Tired and scared
Surprised to see
How well I fared

Not even a scratch
Or nasty smells
To be honest
Nothing more to tell

I'm going back
To sleep away
This nasty dream
Of yesterday

I'll close my eyes
For one quick nap
And set my book
Down on my lap

It's all so real
So scary, too
To think I'd awake
With more sleeping to do

Small Ideas

If it was all up to me
I would stay two or three
I'd never get old or gray

To have people nearby
Whenever I cry
Do things whenever I say

Life's so outta sight
And I'm always right
To small to make a mistake

I'll whine for my lunch
Solid food with a crunch
I want a chocolate milkshake!

Oh yea, I'd like to grow
Put on a bigger show
But why get all angry and mad?

Staying small like a tot
I'll get ooh's, ahh's a lot
I'll always be happy and glad

But then as a baby
I can never plan maybes
I'll be this or one of them

That's OK with me
I'm still only three
The biggest I'm getting is ten!

HappyJack Publishing
P.O. Box 30363 • Middleburg Heights, Ohio 44130